GOYA

by
José Manuel Pita Andrade

photography
Eleonor Domínguez Ramírez

MADRID
1981

Translated by:
Patricia S. Parrent

CONTENTS

Page

INTRODUCTION   5
PERSONAL AND ARTISTIC CHARACTER 10
   His Birth and Studies (1746-1771) 10
   The Road to Fame (1771-1780) 12
   Triumph Among Nobles and Kings (1780-1795) ... 14
   His Encounter with the Duchess of Alba (1795-
      1797) 19
   The Conflict Between Two Centuries (1797-1808) 23
   The Crisis of the War (1808-1814) 28
   In the Court of Ferdinand VII (1814-1824) 32
   His Exile and Death (1824-1828) 36
Notes 39
Bibliography 42
Black and White Illustrations 43
Color Plates 46

INTRODUCTION

If an absurd cataclysm should erase all trace of the man Goya, yet leave his works intact, critics would find as their only common denominator their Spanishness; their other qualities would cause these works to be attributed to different and quite diverse artists, who weren't even contemporaries.

Sánchez Cantón

The quote above, from one of the best authorities on Goya (1), starts things off in an attempt to express, in a few pages, the nature of the greatest genius in painting produced by Europe in the 18th century. No artist has expressed himself using such diverse and even contradictory styles, appearing—to add to the paradox—during one of the drabbest periods in Spanish painting and maturing, as well, in an atmosphere most contrary to his temperament. Due to all this, it is an extremely complex task to sum up the human characteristics of the master who, thanks to an unbounded personality, transcended his times and prepared the way for new trends. No one among those born at the beginning of the contemporary age played such a decisive role in the birth and development of modern painting.

Thanks to his long life, Goya was a witness to the transcendental events which served as the threshold for the world of our times. He experienced the ideological crisis which was the prologue to the French Revolution; he closely followed the tragic episodes which took place after the storming of the Bastille; he was an eye-witness, on the national scene, at the corrupt court of Charles IV; he experienced the dramatic days of the War of Independence; he was acquainted with the tyrannical government of Ferdinand VII and, finally, when he was almost eighty, he chose the road to exile. On the border between two centuries, his life and works take on a special symbolic value. The artist and the man are reflected in paintings and drawings of singular testimonial importance, but even so this does not mean that the vision he offers of his times is not extremely personal and at times impassioned. But passion in Goya is the vehicle for an enthusiasm which seems youthful because it is projected toward the future. The enormous feeling of humanity which his works contain is a result. Looking at them, we sense an emotional tension which makes us look for a background where the figure of the artist is wrapped in a cloak of mystery. This reality which is insinuated and that which is perceived in some texts and documents have caused Goya's biography to be interpreted from the first, due to the stimulus of Romanticism, with large doses of imagination. No other painter gave rise to so many "romanticized lives." Alongside these, his "legend" began to coalesce.

There is room in Goya's biography for the most diverse opinions. Some remember him in the critical years of the Napoleonic invasion as a great patriot; others say he was a Francophile. There are those who praise his religious feelings and those who celebrate him as a freethinker. He has been called the "painter-philosopher"—even discovering in his works the strangest symbols for concealing his thoughts. And as a reaction against these ideas, there has been a desire to accent the vulgarity which can be recognized in the themes of some of his engravings. His relationship with the Duchess of Alba gave rise to the most picturesque rumors. The most contradictory postures have been adopted not only by the "romanticizers," but also by respected critics. Polemics are possible because though we know a lot about Goya's life, some fundamental aspects of his personality escape us.

His correspondence has been published only partially up to now and, what is more serious, some paragraphs of his letters, which could change the image of the artist fabricated by his biographer, have been suppressed. So it happened, for example, with information given by Francisco Zapater using correspondence between his uncle, Martín, and the painter. It is true that this important pamphlet tried, in 1868, to combat works by Mantheron and Iriarte printed in France in 1858 and 1867. As Lafuente Ferrari has correctly observed in a masterly study, the two French writers, "true initiators of the Goya bibliography, have been up to this point scapegoats imprecated by Spanish biographers, polemicists more intent on picking on their picturesque errors than on appreciating the information worthy of belief which they included about the master and which contributed toward preserving invaluable memories which would have been lost without them." (2)

If Goya critics and biographers often expressed themselves in passionate terms, it was because we experience in him a profound disruption of values which affected the concept of art in a fundamental way. But these authors were interested above all in the extra-artistic attitudes adopted by the master in relation to the ideological movements of his time. The Frenchmen present Goya as a critic of the society of his time. Iriarte, according to Lafuente, made our artist the "incarnation of the revolutionary spirit...

a sort of Spanish Rousseau; in a somewhat jocular tone, he begins his work saying he wants to show the role that the philosophical Goya played in the ideological movement of his century." (3) This way of interpreting the personality of a man who was above all a painter does not keep us from collecting early opinions from beyond the Pyrenees, from the strictly artistic viewpoint. Setting aside those of Viardot (only a decade after Goya's death), and Théophile Gautier, we recall some words by the great poet and critic, Baudelaire: "Goya's great merit lies in creating life-like monsters. His monsters are born credible, harmonious. No one has delved deeper than Goya into the feeling of the possible absurdity. All those contortions, those bestial faces, those diabolical grimaces are permeated with humanity... The borderline between the real and the fantastic is impossible for us to apprehend; it is a hazy frontier which the subtlest of analysts would not be capable of demarcating; to such a degree is art natural and transcendental at the same time." (4)

Though thanks to Zapater Goya's image was first depicted in Spain with conservative features, we find curious a *Civil calendar... with the martyred saints, defenders of Independence and Liberty...* printed in Madrid in 1869, in which is found "St. Francisco Goya y Lucientes, famous painter and noted patriot... one of the most illustrious victims of the despotic reign of Ferdinand VII." Thus was our painter cannonized, as Lafuente has informed us. (5) To this text could be added others from the 19th century which appeared in Spain with differing points of view. We do not have room here to discuss works such as those by Cruzada Villaamil (1870), Lefort (1887), the Count of La Viñaza (1887) and Araujo (1896). Let us say that since an important monographic exhibition held in Madrid in 1900, works discussing the personality of the genius from Aragón continually appear. The commemoration of the centennials of his death (1928) and of his birth (1946) were good occasions for exhibitions and studies of great interest. In the entire world this artist, so exceptional for so many reasons, never ceases to be praised. (6)

Since fame smiled on Goya while he was still alive, he had to let himself be surrounded by students and assistants who must have collaborated more than once on the execution of his works. After his death, imitators sprang up. In Spain the most worthy were those who knew how to develop painting in the "bravura style," with a completely fluid technique and themes whose direct antecedents were the master's genre paintings. On an inferior and contemptible level are the forgeries which started appearing in the 19th century due to the enthusiasm which his paintings aroused. In any event, Goya's popularity has not fallen off for a moment since. When analyzing his life and work, it is indispensable to take into account not only the documentary testimony (some very important discoveries have been made in recent decades), but also critical opinions of people like Ortega y Gasset who though they were not directly involved in art history, were attracted to the overwhelming personality of the artist. (7)

PERSONAL AND ARTISTIC CHARACTER

It is interesting to follow Goya's life during more than eight decades to perceive the presence of the flesh and blood man, with his weaknesses and whims, his desire for advancement and enjoyment of the material wealth he acquired, his occasional rebellions and his concessions to the cajoling of fortune. Though we don't accept the legend, at times it will be useful to recall it. And it will also be worthwhile to measure the affects which circumstances had on his works. The letters to his friend Zapater are often brimming over with disagreement with his times. The extraordinary innovations, pioneering and inventiveness manifest in his paintings, drawings and engravings best indicate the measure of his genius.

His Birth and Studies (1746-1771)

Francisco de Goya y Lucientes was born March 30, 1746, in Fuendetodos, a little town in the province of Zaragoza. His father, a resident of the capital, was a gilder. His mother had relatives who farmed in that small town. We do not know the reason the family moved, nor how long they lived there. But we must imagine Francisco's childhood in those drought-ridden lands where, legend has it, his artistic instincts were precociously awakened. It is said that at the age of 12 he decorated the church reliquary. At 14 he was already in Zaragoza and perhaps by then had begun his apprenticeship with José Luzán, a mediocre painter but a distinguished teacher of artists, for he also trained the Bayeu Brothers. But the Aragonese period didn't last very long because in 1763 Goya was already in Madrid. On December 4th his name is mentioned in the San Fernando Fine Arts Academy records as a candidate for one of five stipends for studies in Rome; but the awards went to other mediocre applicants. In 1766 the Academy proved elusive once more, and perhaps with reason, because the genius' temperament had a hard time adjusting to the absurd examination topics. Nonetheless, the move from Aragón to Castile did serve to broaden Goya's horizons. He arrived at the Court shortly after Charles III was proclaimed King of Spain. The monarch, during his years in Naples, had been interested in the Neoclassical movement. In the sixties, and in part due to his influence, the creations appearing at the Court had to follow closely rigorous formulas arising from the picturesque Academic tests. While recalling artistic events, it is worth remembering the presence in Madrid of two quite different artists: the Venetian Giovanni Battista Tiepolo, full of Baroque lyricism, and the Bohemian Anton Raffael Mengs, with a fame and power which would allow him to impose all the dogma of Neoclassicism.

Contact with the atmosphere of Madrid was interrupted by a stay in Italy. Sánchez Cantón thinks that Goya must have made his first trip out of Spain between 1769 and 1771. Due to the impact which certain French pictures had on our artist, he suspects that the trip was made by land. Thus Goya achieved the goal offered as a prize by the San Fernando Academy. A declaration of his confirms his presence "in Rome, which he reached and where he lived at his own expense." This fact is backed up by the delivery of a painting, *Hannibal Contemplating the Alps,* to the Academy at Parma. The picture didn't win a prize, but at least it got six votes. Some works known to be from this brief Italian period help us imagine how Goya made his living, but they do not reveal a master's hand, but that of an artist in formation, open to the influences of the Italian settcento and vacillating between Baroque and Neoclassical aesthetics.

The Road to Fame (1771-1780)

The age of 25 serves as the starting point for a rising trajectory, interrupted by some crises which helped to temper Goya's creative genius. In October of 1771 he was commissioned to do some sketches for the choir vault in the Pilar Basilica at Zaragoza. He remained in Aragón three years, though with a Madrilenian parenthesis in 1773; while in Madrid he married Josefa Bayeu, the sister of Francisco, a painter who probably contributed greatly to our artist's finding a definitive niche in the Court. To the commission for the Pilar church must be added others for the Cartuja de Aula Dei, the Count of Gabarra's Palace, the Sobradiel Palace and for churches at Muel and Remolins. These paintings, with very special exceptions, are not overly important in Goya's overall production.

His activity in Madrid is inaugurated by the portrait of the *Count of Miranda,* in the Lázaro Galdiano Museum, and above all by his acceptance as a painter of cartoons for the Royal Tapestry Factory. Thanks to Valentín de Sambricio's studies, we have details of his work distributed in various periods of unequal length from 1774 to 1792. The good offices of his brother-in-law operated positively so that Goya found a place in the royal factories; Mengs' favorable intervention was probably not lacking either. The documents preserved let us see how Goya progressed beyond other mediocre artists, but it would be unfair to say that his paintings stood out from the first due to their quality. There are notable differences between various cartoons, and as the years go by, greater mastery of the brushwork can be observed. There are 63 cartoons in all, not counting some replicas of sketches. (9) When appraising this work, we should not forget that it is, to a large extent, secondary in nature, since the cartoon was only a means for achieving, through the threads of the tapestry, the final work. The genre themes surely pleased Goya, letting him express himself with great vitality. The markedly popular accent of the scenes has many antecedents in 17th-century Flemish painting. When Jacob Vandergoten the Elder began his work in Madrid in 1720, the looms—at Philip V's wish—produced more than anything copies of Teniers and Wouwermans. Among works from before 1780, *The Quail Hunt* is one of Goya's first cartoons; it was delivered in 1775. Two years later he does *The Parasol,* reproduced here.

In this decade's artistic trajectory, the "discovery" of Velázquez must have been important. A period of convalescence in 1778 was used, according to Sánchez Cantón's guess, to do engravings of some of the famous canvases by the painter from Seville. This period ends with Goya's first attempt to become a painter to the King, which had as a prologue an encounter with the royal family. In January, 1779, he writes to Zapater: "If I had more time, I'd tell you about the honor done to me by the King, the

— 13

Prince and the Princess, whom the grace of God allowed me to show four paintings, and I kissed their hands, a stroke of fortune I had never had before, and I tell you I couldn't ask for more concerning their liking my pictures, in view of the pleasure they felt seeing them, and the King was more satisfied than their Highnesses." The letter ends with these significant words: "Now I begin to have more important and ill-tempered enemies." In June Mengs died in Rome and a month later Goya applied for the vacant position as painter to the King. Nonetheless, in reply to the request, and though recognizing Goya to be "an applied professor, of talent and spirit, who promises more progress in his art," it was proposed that since "there is no urgency nor any noticeable dearth of painters... for royal service... the individual in question may keep on with the paintings used for the tapestry factory, endeavoring to do his best with these." (10)

Triumph Among Nobles and Kings (1780-1795)

On May 7, 1780, Goya was compensated for the reverses suffered the previous year by being named a member of the San Fernando Academy. He painted, with this motive, *The Crucifixion,* in the Prado, completely identified with the Neoclassical doctrine and stylistically very close to Mengs. Did he wish to pay homage with this canvas to the memory of his protector? The honor received did not keep Goya's prestige from suffering when he did some new paintings for the Pilar Cathedral in Zaragoza. The canons were not satisfied with the sketches he presented for the squinches in the vaults. A letter to Zapater dated July 25, 1781, informs us of a new job for the San Francisco el Grande Church in Madrid which may have served as compensation for the Zaragoza incident. In this letter may be sensed the tensions, enthusiasm and—why not say so?—pride which were developing in Goya's life. Nonetheless, the picture *St. Bernardine of Siena Preaching Before Alfonso V of Aragón* was nothing special, as even the Minister Floridablanca himself commented. We possess, however, a valuable document about it which lets us know Goya's aesthetic ideas at that time: it alludes to the narrowness of the picture's proportions and the need to develop its composition in a pyramidal sense. (11) Other religious works painted shortly thereafter, such as those of the Calatrava College in Salamanca (unfortunately lost), the ones at Valdemoro, Valladolid and Valencia would complete Goya's image as a painter of devotional canvases in this period, reaching a level of achievement which we should not disdain.

In 1783 Goya must have felt personal satisfaction when he was given the chance to do a portrait of the *Count of Floridablanca*; the work, in which the artist appears showing a small picture to the minister, turned out rather contrived. More important was the acquaintance struck up that same year with the unfortunate brother of the King, the Infante Don Luis, shunned at the Court due to his morganatic marriage (at 49, to Doña María Teresa Vallabriga, who was 17). His life was spent between Arenas de San Pedro, Boadilla del Monte and Chinchón. The picture depicting the Infante's family possesses an anti-courtly, profoundly bourgeois character; this is the first sign of what the Spanish middle class would be like in the 19th century.

Goya continued to add to his list of clients and friends, portraying the famous architect *Don Ventura Rodríguez* and working for various noble houses, with the Duke of Osuna's standing out over all the others. Sánchez Cantón fixes "1785 as the beginning of the most brilliant period in Goya's life; the brightest hour." (12) The contact with the duke and duchess resulted in an important series of pictures which decorated a lovely mansion in "Alameda de Osuna."

Goya's "brightest hour" is marked by a promotion at the San Fernando Academy, since in 1785 he was named Assistant Director of Painting. Thus the bitter memeories of Zaragoza and even the sadness caused by his father's death in 1782 begin to fade. It is worth referring to a moment in his private life, via a letter written to Zapater, because in it may be perceived his regret of follies committed during his youth. When he condoled with his friend for the death of a sister, he said, "I found consolation in my belief that she was very good and will have found salvation, but we, who have been such rascals, must mend our ways in the time left to us." Concerning the pastimes which occupy him during these years, the main one is probably hunting. We should indicate that he accompanied the Infante Don Luis twice and from other indications we know that he went hunting quite frequently.

An important advance was made in 1786. In a letter dated July 7th, Goya joyfully informed his friend: "Now I'm a painter to the King, with a 15,000 reales stipend..." Thus he was continually achieving honors. To all these things must be added economic prosperity. It is logical that he would feel like moving to a better home and exchanging his two-wheeled carriage (a "sulky" with which he suffered a fall which left him temporarily lame) for a four-wheeled berlin drawn by two mules.

We will not tire the reader with details of Goya's

activities in these years. His commissions and clients from noble families, institutions of such importance as the San Carlos Bank, convents and churches continue to multiply. Now he has more than sufficient prestige and fame. Knowing his attraction to royalty and nobility, we can imagine the satisfaction with which he must have painted the Velazquez-like portrait of *Charles III,* preserved in the Bank of Spain. On December 14, 1788, the King died and on April 25th of the following year Goya obtained the title of First Painter to the King, willingly granted by Charles IV and María Luisa. Thus, in that decisive year in world history, with the storming of the Bastille, Goya achieved the highest-ranking title to which a court painter could aspire.

Before referring to the serious crisis which ruins his health, we should recall Goya's activity, during the period concerned, as a painter at the Royal Tapestry Factory. Between 1786 and 1792 we record 24 cartoons. Among them we find the most famous ones, for example, *The Grape Harvest* and *Blindman's Buff,* which is reproduced here. But we should also recall the fortunate composition of *The San Isidro Meadow* (which we only know from the sketch). An enrichment of subject matter is affirmed by the satirical notes shown in the scene of *The Wedding,* the animation of *The Dummy* and *The Stilt Walkers,* and the unusual values which show the large *Wounded Bricklayer* to be a forerunner of social painting, with a burlesque counterpoint in a small sketch, the *Drunk Bricklayer.* Also worth noting from the technical point of view is a greater freedom in the use of colors.

In 1793 we reach a critical date in Goya's life: that of the affliction which will leave him deaf. There is no doubt that this was one of his most serious illnesses and

that Sánchez Cantón has studied it correctly. (13)   It is
most probable that Goya's life was in grave danger.   The
seriousness of it was demonstrated by an extremely long
absence from the Academy: from September 2, 1792 until
July 11th of the following year.   On one hand, his illness
seems related to a tense time in his life, with trips to An-
dalusia, evidently in search of a remedy for his ruined
health; on the other, there are indications of events whose
ultimate meaning we do not know, but which raise the
suspicion that the youthful follies decried 11 years earlier
had been repeated.   The circumstances of this illness are
intriguing and the tone of a letter from Zapater to Francisco Bayeu is perplexing: "Goya's... own lack of reflec-
tion has gotten him into this; but it is necessary to look
on him with the compassion which his misfortune calls
for, and as a sick man to whom one must offer all possible
relief, as you have done."

The illness, or ills, which the artist suffered had a
serious consequence which affected his life and even his
works: deafness.   The loss of his hearing initiated a
violent separation between Goya and the world around
him.   Though many years of life remained to him, from
now on a sharp turn in his character was produced which
influenced his view of art in the future; his fits of ill-
humor, irritability, and nonconformism must have been
accentuated.   But in an odd manner the illnes is con-
nected to another event which would give rise to a fantasy
of many biographers.   We are speaking of an affair exag-
gerated by legend but whose basis in reality may not be
doubted: one which opens a new and brief chapter in
the painter's life.

His Encounter with the Duchess of Alba (1795-1797)

A minute and impartial analysis of the facts would possibly disappoint many readers. In Ezquerra del Bayo's suggestive monograph, *Goya and the Duchess of Alba,* many hypotheses have been put forth which are just that, no more —hypotheses—and the enigmas remain, in spite of various later attempts to clear them up. A rapid sketch of María del Pilar Teresa Cayetana de Silva y Alvarez de Toledo will help bring the matter into focus.

Baptized in Madrid in 1762 (she was given no less than 31 names), she was the daughter of the heir to the Duchy of Alba, the Duke of Huéscar, who died before his parents did; her grandfather, Don Fernando de Silva y Alvarez de Toledo, XII Duke of Alba, was extraordinarily important in the Courts of Ferdinand VI and Charles III, playing an important role as the ambassador for our monarchs in Paris. The education of the XIII Duchess of Alba was lacking. It is almost certain that she never attended school and that at home she had no elevated example to follow. Her playmates must have been the servants' children; these childhood acquaintances would explain her constant sympathy for everything "popular," her affection for the humble classes. The scene of her childhood was not only Madrid, but also Piedrahita, where her grandfather had just finished building a lovely palace over the ruins of an ancient castle. In 1770, when she was 8 years old, her father died and the child's future became a serious worry for her grandfather. When she was 11, her marriage to the Marquis of Villafranca was decided on, and in 1775 the ceremony was held at the same time as her mother's second marriage, to the Count of Fuentes.

At the age of 13 we find our little duchess married to

a man who could not be more contrary to her tastes. She liked popular festivities, dances, an exciting life. He preferred a tranquil existence, dedicated to the cultivation of music; we know that he organized concerts with the Infante Don Gabriel and corresponded with Haydn. With these contrasting personalities it's easy to understand if their relationship was not a close one. Anecdotes abound allowing us to suspect frivolous conduct by the Duchess, to whose attractions various texts refer. In 1777 Cayetana's grandfather died, leaving her numerous titles and a large fortune. During a few years we can imagine the XIII Duchess not only occupying a position of the first order on the social scale (she frequented the luxurious gatherings at the Alameda de Osuna), but also attending the "popular" festivals, of which she was so fond. Far from the royal family, her fame nonetheless spread everywhere. Langle wrote in 1784: "The Duchess of Alba doesn't have a hair on her head which doesn't kindle desire. Nothing in the world is as beautiful as she... when she passes by everyone looks out his window and even the children stop playing to watch her." Five years later Moldenhaver referred to the frivolity of her habits. Lady Holland spoke of "her beauty, popularity, grace, wealth and lineage." Need we add the laudatory testimony of other poets of the times, such as Quintana and Meléndez Valdés? Perhaps a second-rate writer had adulatory intentions when he considered her "the new Venus of Spain." But we can have no doubt that she was attractively good-looking. (14)

In spite of all Ezquerra del Bayo's optimistic arguments, the first sure contact between Goya and the Duchess of Alba does not occur until 1795, when the painter was about to turn 50 and Cayetana was 33. The earliest documentary evidence dates from that year; it is a letter to

Zapater, dated, jokingly, in London in 1800. In it we read: "It would be better for you to come and help me paint that Alba woman, who yesterday showed up at my studio wanting me to do a study of her head, and she's gotten her way; ...I am also supposed to do a full-length portrait of her..." After that study must have come, then, the magnificent canvas in the Liria Palace which is reproduced here. In 1796 an unexpected event took place: the death of the Marquis of Villafranca. On becoming a widow, the Duchess moved to an estate of hers, near Sanlúcar de Barrameda; we are referring to the famous Doñana Wildlife Preserve, the splendid park famous for the many birds nesting there. Sánchez Cantón has been able to document Goya's presence there, though it has not been possible to ascertain how long he was absent from Madrid. He is not listed as attending the Academy board meetings from October 2, 1796, until April 30th of the next year, when "he resigns his position as Director of Painting due to his repeated indispositions and especially due to his resultant deafness." (15)

Did Goya only go to Sanlúcar in search of a peaceful spot to recover his waning health? One needn't be a gossip to imagine other motives of a sentimental nature. The drawings preserved from that trip suggest something more than days filled with serene peace. In several of them the Duchess of Alba appears, sometimes portrayed with intimate freedom, at others (*The Dream of Lies and Fickleness, Volaverunt...*) having butterfly wings. Could these scenes be the symbol of an amorous disillusionment? Indications lead us to suspect frustration.

To recall the drawings from the so-called Sanlúcar Album is equivalent to beginning the history of the execution of *Los Caprichos,* which starting from these drawings and enriched with others, were engraved in the final years of the century. I believe that the psychological climate which drew Goya's life to the shores of the Guadalquivir can justify better than anything else a work which brings us into a world filled with visions, with satires, where all the principles of Neoclassical aesthetics are rejected in order to penetrate the unfathomable spheres of dreams and nightmares. Leaving aside their moralizing intention, perhaps these drawings should be related to texts of the period. Goya's contemporaries such as the fablists Samaniego and Iriarte could in some cases help in understanding this subject matter. The examples reproduced here are quite expressive.

Goya must have consoled the slight grief which the death of her husband caused the Duchess of Alba. But the strong personality of each of these individuals makes us think that they did not remain together for every long and may even have broken off in a violent manner. Even restraining the imagination, solid motives exist to venture likely a brief, episodic, amorous entanglement, while conjectures about a prolonged passion broken off by Cayetana's death seem to have no basis. What we know about the artist's life during the last years of the century does not match up with the Duchess' activities in the last 5 years of her life. After Sanlúcar there are allusions in letters to the Queen to a possible pursuit by Godoy, and above all there is a strong suspicion of an affair with Lt. General Don Antonio Cornel. By 1800 the Duchess' reputation had suffered quite a bit. We can imagine with what satisfaction María Luisa must have written to her favorite, Godoy: "That Alba woman... is only skin and bones." She died at the age of 40, on July 23, 1802. Charles IV ordered an investigation to see if she had been poisoned.

When the body was exhumed a century and a half later, an analysis showed no traces of arsenic. (16)

After the above, the reader is probably disillusioned that nothing has been said about the *Majas* in relation to the Duchess; they surely have nothing to do with her. Due to their style they may be dated, at the earliest, around 1800. The affair lasted at the most from 1795 to 1797, beginning, pictorially, with the portrait in the Liria Palace and ending with another extremely lovely one preserved in the Hispanic Society in New York. The stormy details of this love which probably had a serene ending will never be known.

The Conflict Between Two Centuries (1797-1808)

If we pick up the threads of Goya's life again, we will start with 1797, because some portraits from this year make us see that he had returned to work even though, not counting emotional problems, his health was not good. We know from a letter that on March 22, 1798, he was ill and he must have been totally deaf from what can be deduced from the Academy records. The experiences he went through must have produced the state of crisis reflected in his works: the period we are discussing begins with paintings of witches that he does for the Countess-Duchess of Benavente and religious works of such importance as the decoration of the San Antonio de la Florida ceiling. The subjects, so diverse, possess a common point in their bold technique. All this helps us to anticipate a grave moral crisis which, as if that weren't enough, is mixed up with politics, in a Spain which is on the brink of the most tragic events.

To sketch Goya's personality in these years, it is indispensable to present the political atmosphere in the sincerest of terms. After the triumph of the French Revolution the figure of Napoleon dominated all Europe, acting in the Spanish Court through Godoy, who dreamed of being King of the Algarve. Inside the country, the outlook could not be more pessimistic: Charles IV lets his wife María Luisa and her favorite handle the destiny of a poorly-governed Spain immersed in continual palace intrigues. Prince Ferdinand is the symbol of hope for some well-meaning Spaniards and he boldly conspires against his father. Thus a series of years with painful memories passes, culminating in the Aranjuez uprising of March 19, 1808. Godoy is overthrown when the intervention of French troops in Spain's historical destiny turns out to be inevitable. The ineptness of our rulers would bring as a consequence the uprising of the Spanish people on the 2nd of May.

Goya, with his deafness and chronic illness, was not unaffected by this situation which doubtlessly must have depressed him and influenced his future attitudes. The position as court painter was a good one from which to follow the palace intrigues very closely. Paradoxically, it did not fail to flatter the artist to know that he was highly esteemed by those monarchs and their unworthy minister. María Luisa speaks of the painter in almost familiar terms in her letters. Our man, who was not immune to courtly vanities, must have felt more than uncomfortable in an atmosphere where he was honored, but which contradicted his innermost beliefs. Goya's ideological position must be analyzed in relation to all the ideas which gave birth to the French Revolution and whose ferment acted powerfully in Spain, above all in certain intellectual circles to which the painter was no stranger. A man of exceptional stature, Jovellanos, a friend of Goya's and a victim of Godoy's paltriness, displays a similar posture. In spite of all that has been said, the years in the 19th century preceding the War of Independence were still of "productive well-being," to use the words of Sánchez Cantón. Goya bought a house in 1803 and generously presented it to his son Javier on his marriage. Goya's finances must have been strengthened during these years by the execution of a growing number of portraits. (17)

This important period definitively reveals Goya's genius. His full maturity and above all a creative impulse lead him to become the great initiator of contemporary painting. If the affliction which left him deaf had robbed him of his life, his place in the history of art would be a very secondary one. It is after the age of 50 that his most incisive works, the ones fullest of imagination, those which best show the incredible stylistic departures of which we spoke at the beginning, arise.

Following Goya's extravagances with the Duchess of Alba, let us evoke, as a cleansing influence, some religious works. Why not link the Santa Cueva paintings in Cádiz to his Andalusian visit, as an epilogue? These canvases constitute, even in their form, the best prologue to the admirable work done in the San Antonio de la Florida Hermitage in 1798, where with incisive and expressive figures Goya is proven an exceptional decorator. Other religious works of great pictorial importance are the *Pope St. Gregory,* preserved in the Romantic Museum and *The Betrayal of Christ,* in the Toledo Cathedral. When this canvas was restored some years ago, its extraordinary chromatic qualities were brought to light; the face of Christ, impassive midst a series of gesticulating and deformed heads, introduces us into the strange world of monstrous beings which capture the artist's attention from now on; the light, coming from the left, possesses a strange unreality.

Touching on profane themes, it is worth insisting on technical coincidences with works of a religious type. The large tapestry cartoons are now followed by tiny, small-format paintings among which an important place is occupied by those painted for the Alameda de Osuna. Truly admirable are the two witches scenes from the Lázaro Galdiano Museum, reproduced here. But this theme had its most decisive material realization in the drawings which gave life to the series of etchings known as *Los Caprichos*. This aspect, so important, of Goya's production is limited to the last decade of the century. With his illness as the motive, on January 4, 1794, he had sent to D. Bernardo de Iriarte 11 paintings done, as he confessed, "in order to distract my imagination, mortified by the consideration of my afflictions." About this time he may have begun the copper plates done after the inevitable preliminary drawings. We already know how important his meeting with the Duchess of Alba was in the elaboration of the "Sanlúcar Album." The fruit of the labor of these years materialized in the famous *Caprichos*. The series had been finished in 1797, but the first news of their appearance is a receipt made out to the Countess-Duchess of Benavente, and dated two years later. In an advertisement in the "Diario de Madrid," its content was explained in these words: "...Since the author is convinced that the censure of human errors and vices... can also be the subject of painting, he has chosen as appropriate topics for his work, from among the multitude of extravagances and blunders common to all civil society, and from among the vulgar frauds and worries allowed by custom, ignorance or interest, those which he considered most apt to supply material for ridicule and which at the same time stirred the imagination of the craftsman." These sentences are enough to clear up the meaning of the 80 engravings which make up the collection. It is logical that it would be quite successful from the very first and though its distribution produced negative reactions, such as a denunciation to the Inquisition, the series contributed decisively to assuring the artist's fame outside of his own country.

During the last years of the 18th century and the first years of the 19th, Goya's activity as a portrait artist was very important. The likenesses of *The Marquise of Lazán, The Archbishop Company* and *Leandro Fernández de Moratín,* reproduced here, are splendid. We should also recall those of *The Architect Villanueva,* in the San Fernando Academy and *Jovellanos,* one of the clearest-sighted men of the times, acquired by the Prado Museum. Alongside works such as these, those revealing his activity as a court painter occupy an important spot; besides great artistic value, they possess decisive interest from the historical angle. In the last two years of the century, in 1799 and 1800, Goya worked indefatigably, doing portraits of the monarchs with standing as well as equestrian poses. In them may be seen once more his taste for veracity, not omitting certain features which were even unflattering to his models. But the most ambitious iconographical testimony about the royalty is contained in *The Family of Charles IV,* done in Aranjuez in the spring of 1800. The work, which marks a moment of plenitude in Goya's artistic trajectory, possesses an instructive historical significance. (18)

Other pictures also contain an evocative forcefulness.

That of the Prince of Peace, *Godoy,* painted in 1801, recalls the events which culminated in the famous "War of Oranges" against Portugal. In contrast to it is the one of the lovable figure of his wife, *The Countess of Chinchón,* daughter of the Infante Don Luis, who lived in a profoundly isolated situation in the Court of Charles IV. Goya knew how to reflect all the affection he felt for this individual, tinged with melancholy and timidity. From the circle of noble personalities, we should also emphasize the portraits of the *Count of Fernán Núñez* and of the *Marquis of San Adrián,* with notes of distinction and refinement worthy of the best English painting; the portrait dated 1805 of the *Marquise of Santa Cruz,* done in the Neoclassical style, with the figure reclining and holding a lyre (decorated, in fact, with a swastika), using the same compositional technique predominant in *The Majas,* which for stylistic reasons may correspond to this moment.

The Crisis of the War (1808-1814)

The years of the War of Independence situate us in one of the most difficult to judge periods in Goya's life. Even today, his attitude toward Napoleon is generally defined based on the ideological position of the artist's biographer. Lafuente has already observed how Goya was tugged and pulled from one side to the other almost from the moment of his death. It is true that the painter's attitude toward the French could not be argued about if there did not exist abundant evidence both pro and con. Let's sum up one and the other before we offer an opinion. Those who make Goya a Francophile can point out his friendship with intellectuals who not only sympathized, but also collaborated with the invaders: such as Moratín, Meléndez Valdés, Bravo del Rivero, etc. Goya swore allegiance to the new regime as the head of a household. In 1810 he went to the San Fernando Academy to pay his respects to the Marquis of Almenara, named the institution's protector by King Joseph (Bonaparte). In 1811 he received from the intruder king the so-called "Royal Order of Spain," which the Madrilenians had humorously re-named the "order of the eggplant." Goya added his signature after the words, "I swear to be ever faithful to honor and the King," following the stipulated formula. It cannot be denied that between 1809 and 1810, from December 23rd to January 27th, he painted an *Allegory of Madrid with Joseph I,* due to a commission from his friend Don Tadeo Bravo del Rivero, with no economic problems as an excuse for this collaboration: for his money problems could not have been very serious. As painter to Joseph Bonaparte, he participated in the selection of paintings for the great Napoleon Museum in Paris. Even more circumstances could be recalled in favor of his being a Francophile.

In spite of everything, once the war was over, Goya could defend himself without difficulty to obtain acquittal. Those who support his ultra-patriotism are correct in recognizing the minimal value of oaths of adhesion to a regime or person in such exceptional circumstances. They also insist on how careful Goya was not to wear in public the decoration he'd been awarded. When he chose the 50 paintings to be sent to France, he tried to select ones not distinguished for their quality. To be added to this is the undeniable fact that in these bitter years he drew and painted scenes of war portrayed in the brutalest manner, though he emphasized more the suffering and heroism

—29

of the Spaniards than the violence committed by the French.

Without accumulating more arguments pro or con, it is clear that the artist maintained an indecisive attitude. He neither resolutely faced up to the invaders, refusing to serve them, as did Jovellanos while he was alive, nor did he frankly show himself to be in favor of the Francophiles. Goya, just because he was an artistic genius, did not necessarily have to behave like a hero. Without doubt, a factor of capital importance played a part in his vacillating position: the battle between two principles. One was that the invaders brought in liberal ideas with which Goya sympathized; and the other, that thus the Spanish people were placed under domination. Doesn't Napoleon, perhaps, present us with this type of contradiction? Didn't he want to be in charge of spreading thoughout Europe the ideas of liberty germinated by the French Revolution and which he paradoxically wanted to spread by force? It is worth recalling the well-known anecdote about Beethoven, who had dedicated his Third Symphony, the Eroica, to Bonaparte, but withdrew the dedication when he heard that the Frenchman had crowned himself Emperor.

We can understand Goya's actions and reactions between 1808 and 1814 much better as the result of a tremendous spiritual crisis. On the other hand, the reward the patriots received after their brave battle can only seem tremendously ironic: a monarch who after effusively congratulating Napoleon on his victories in Spain, returned to the Peninsula in order to impose the most shameful absolutist forms of government. The war years brought, within the family circle, the death of Josefa Bayeu on June 20, 1812, after having drawn up a will with her husband the year before in which Francisco Javier, the only child from the marriage, was named the exclusive heir to the remaining goods of both.

On analyzing the works corresponding to this period, we may observe how pictures of great imaginative content began to flourish, though a portrait or two show that Goya did not stop cultivating, if even to a very limited extent, this productive genre. In the above-mentioned *Allegory,* the effigy of the intruder King is see inside an oval (after several repaintings, today only the words "Second of May" can be seen); thus Goya became the painter of four kings. Before this he had finished an *Equestrian Portrait of Ferdinand VII,* while later (1812 and 1814) he did portraits, also on horseback, of *Wellington* and *Palafox.* A religious painting done during the war is worth recalling: the *Assumption of the Virgin,* painted for the church at Chinchón, where Goya's brother Camilo was a parishioner. The other works correspond to different stimuli. After the 2nd of May, the artist withdrew from the outside world; this is probably when he did the five admirable little paintings in the San Fernando Academy, four of which are reproduced and discussed here, and in which the painter of the "bravura style" is revealed.

All in all, the most important chapter in Goya's production in the war years and those immediately afterward consists of the drawings, sketches and canvases wich serve as vigorous testimony to these same events. These works are also exponents of one of the most serious moral crises of the artist, now in his sixties. The events of the War of Independence, which had a profound impact on his spirit, left a mark on his artistic production in a different manner. Perhaps the most direct chronicle of the tragedy should be looked for in the drawings, surely engravings by 1810, forming a series of 82 plates, which make up the cycle, *The Disasters of War*. If in the genre paintings Goya could find at times a kind of escape, in these depictions would materialize the pain felt in view of the unequal battle of the Spanish people against the French troops, but objectified and universalized. They are a tremendous allegation against war in its broadest sense. No intention is seen in them to divide the participants up into "good guys" and "bad guys." The way is opened up for a new concept of heroism and patriotism which would not be much in harmony with the artificial theatrical poses which usually thrive on such occasions.

The sketches done between 1808 and 1814, easily hidden, offer the most direct interpretation of the historical events. Nonetheless, paintings are not lacking which should be inserted in this period. Thus two small pictures preserved in El Escorial which recall the *Powder Factory* and *The Rifle Munitions Factory,* according to the inscription in the Tardienta Mountains (Aragón), and the one exhibited in the Prado with the title of *The Colossus* or *Panic,* with a violently dramatic feeling. But all the war testimony submitted up to now pales before the extremely famous paintings discussed in the commentaries and painted in 1814, evoking the events of 1808 in Madrid: *The Charge of the Mamelukes and the Imperial Guard in the Puerta del Sol* and *The Executions.* (19)

In the Court of Ferdinand VII (1814-1824)

When the War of Independence ends and Ferdinand VII returns to Spain, Goya is 68. Until April of 1815, he lived through the episodes of the "purge" free from blame and with all the judgements favorable. But, with the troubled political atmosphere of the times, he must have been uncomfortable from the first in the service of the new monarch. Everything makes us suspect a progressive separation from the Court. In contrast to certain circumstancial canvases, the works indicating an inner desire for escape and manifesting a technique which is more daring each day seem to be more characteristic of this period.

Thanks to the fortunate discovery of a document by Sánchez Cantón, numerous legends have been refuted concerning Goya's life in a home he owned near the right bank of the Manzanares River, close to the Segovia Bridge. We now know that it was acquired on February 27, 1819, and therefore could not have been the scene of intimate encounters with the Duchess of Alba, nor the point for watching, a bit up the river and not far from the other bank, the executed patriots. (20) On the other hand, knowing the date that the "Deaf Man's Villa" was acquired better prepares us to imagine the emotional state of the artist when he covered the house's walls with the famous Black Paintings.

A careful look at the works from this period will show that Goya, in spite of all the crises, did not remain inactive. But there is only room for a very brief recollection of the main pictures. Those which he did as a portrait artist are represented by several examples, among which stand out those of *Ferdinand VII,* with a disagreeable expression, but admirable from the technical point of view and the one of *The Duke of San Carlos*, reproduced here. On a more personal level, direct and spontaneous are the two *Self-portraits* (1815), in the Prado and in the San Fernando Academy, and the likeness of his grandson *Mariano Goya,* which revives the underlying strata of tenderness in our artist.

In the area of religious painting, worth remembering is the group with *Ss. Justina and Rufina* (1817) at the Seville Cathedral, vituperated by the Count of La Viñaza as "the most profane, worldly and unfortunate of Goya's religious paintings," in spite of its undeniable merits. On the other hand, two canvases done in 1819 for the San Antón Schools reach exceptional heights of religious emotion: *St. Joseph of Calasanz' Last Communion* and *The Prayer in the Garden.* (21) The attention merited by the fiercest series of paintings owed to Goya prevents us from considering other paintings (*The Water Carrier* and *The Knife Sharpener* at Budapest; *The Shipwreck,* belonging to the Marquis of Oquendo; *The Forge,* in the Frick Collection at New York; *The Croup,* in the Marañón Collection, etc.) which are very interesting.

The artist's creative impetus reached its definitive peak in the series of compositions painted on the walls of his country home between February of 1819 and June of 1824. He probably did the work in summer sessions, practically coinciding with the constitutional triennium. Since these works are documented at such a late date, our genius gains in stature, showing himself capable of unprecedented efforts near the age of 75. The *Black Paintings* have been so-named due to their predominant colors, though restoration work done not too long ago has permitted the appreciation of other colors. The series consists of 14 compositions of varying proportions—with horizontally elongated ones predominating—6 of them occupied a room almost 9 meters by more than 5-1/2 meters on the ground floor; the 8 remaining works were found in a room of equal dimensions on the floor above. They were done in oils directly on the wall surface and then were transferred to canvas at the orders of Baron Frederic Emile d'Erlanger, who acquired the property in 1860 and donated the works to the Prado Museum 20 years later. Sánchez Cantón's and Xavier de Salas' thorough study (22) allows an objective evaluation of this great cycle which has so fired the critics' imaginations.

Since they were painted directly onto the walls, it is necessary to admit that Goya must have arranged the compositions in each room following a certain order, but without thus sacrificing his freedom of expression and leaving a very wide margin for changes which were the fruit of momentary or capricious inspirations. Few artists were more rebellious than ours against previously set norms. The *Black Paintings* offer us the most edifying evidence of how artistic creation embodies a process filled with mysterious echoes which the viewer or critic must capture relying on the creation's most external elements. We can never penetrate the inner recesses of Goya's soul to discover the private impulses which made him populate the walls of his home with monsters, witches, hallucinatory mythological figures, Biblical characters and simple mortals. There is no doubt that in each room there coexisted the most diverse themes, and when we speak of an "order," we should only think of the criterion used to distribute the compositions in the two rooms. The separate commentaries on some of the works illustrated here can help us to outline their "Expressionist" characteristics, in the same way that the San Antonio frescos or the *Third of May* developed the pictorial principles of Impressionism.

In the decade concerning us, Goya's activities in the fields of drawing and engraving remain to be discussed, though important doubts exist in relation to the dates of some works. The *Tauromaquia* cycle, masterfully analyzed by Lafuente Ferrari, (23) consists of 40 plates which were put on sale in 1816. Goya contemplates the bullfight with a surprising vigor, variety and drama. The most diverse maneuvers by individuals on foot and on horseback, the vibrant feeling of motion and the extremely free technique, using a red pencil basis, give this series a seal of individuality.

The last of the great engraving cycles was published by the San Fernando Academy in 1863, with the title *Proverbs,* but today it is known more expressively as *Los Disparates* (Follies). They form a collection of 18 plates, plus 5 unpublished ones, brought to light by the magazine "L'Art." These works, probably done at a time very near the *Black Paintings,* are related to them by their ambience.

His Exile and Death (1824-1828)

At the beginning of the Absolutist decade Goya became anxious. The new climate of persecution probably moved him to take measures to protect his person and property. He left his famous "Villa" to his grandson Mariano and stayed hidden for 3 months, until May when a sort of amnesty was proclaimed, in the house of his friend Don José Duaso, who held an important position in the Court of Ferdinand VII. Then at the age of 78, he asked for permission to visit the baths at Plombières, in the Vosges Mountains. The King authorized his exit, but Goya did not head for the famous thermal springs; he went in search of friends and relatives in exile. One of them, Leandro Fernández de Moratín, announced his arrival with these words: "Goya, in fact, arrived deaf, old, crippled and weak, not speaking a word of French and without a servant (no one needed one more than he) and very content and anxious to see the world. He was here three days: two of them he ate with us, as if he were a young student; I begged him to come back in September and not to dawdle in Paris and let winter catch him by surprise, because it would finish him off."

We don't have room here to discuss the curious details related to his trip to France's capital and his stay in Bordeaux, where the artist was watched over by Doña Leocadia Zorrilla, who brought along her children Guillermo and Rosarito Weiss. (25) Goya's relationship with this woman displays a part of his private life not lacking in disagreeable elements, though the daughter, 10 years old, must have stirred Goya's feelings of tenderness. In 1825 he asked once again for the King's leave, this time using as a pretext the baths at Bagneres. In 1826 he made an exhausting journey to Madrid, in spite of his poor health, to settle his affairs, obtaining on June 17th his retirement, with full pay, as Court Painter and also permission to return to France. Without going into the problems created by this trip, and another possible one in the following year, we shall recall the painter's last moments.

In March, 1828, Goya impatiently awaits the arrival of his son Francisco Javier, his daughter-in-law and his grandson Mariano. All indications are that the reason for the trip was the old man's ill health. On the 28th he joyfully greets his daughter-in-law and grandson, and on April 1st he writes to Javier: "I can only tell you that such joy has left me a bit overcome and I am resting in bed. God grant that I may see you when you come and my joy shall be complete." The next day, his saint's day, this slight ailment turned into a hemiplegia, from the description given to Moratín by Doña Leocadia; that day "he awoke at 5 a.m. unable to talk, but he recovered his speech in an hour, and he remained paralyzed on one side. He stayed thus for thirteen days; he recognized everyone up to three hours before his death; he looked at his hand as if stupified; he said he wanted to make a will in our favor and his daughter-in-law told him he had already done so. After this nothing was certain; due to his weakness, he could hardly be understood and was delirious."

Goya died before dawn on April 16, 1828, only a few days after he turned 82. After he died, probably the 20th, his son arrived, quickly settling with poor Doña Leocadia, who bitterly complained of her difficult economic situation. After his death the artist's fame continued to spread unceasingly, thanks to the impact of his work on painters in France and Spain. The story of his descendants continued on a more prosaic level, especially with respect to his bourgeois son Javier and his half-witted grandson Mariano.

In spite of personal problems in his final years, Goya's creativity continued up to the last moment. The admirable portraits of *Don Bautista Muguiro* (1827) and *Don Pío Molina* (1828) let us appreciate his latest technical advances and novelties in coloring—masterful, above all, in *The Milkmaid of Bordeaux,* which can conclude the review of his paintings. His vocation for drawing and engraving was maintained during the Bordeaux period. In 1825 he wrote his friend Ferrer about some new editions. At this time some animal lithographs were done which once again confirm the artist's lack of talent for these subjects; but along with them we should point out the series entitled *The Bulls of Bordeaux,* with 4 prints full of animation and originality. Could Goya's last drawing have been one depicting an old man leaning on two canes and with the significant caption *I'm Still Learning?*

NOTES

1. **Vida y obras de Goya**, p. 2. As we begin our brief sketch of the artist, we'd like to indicate the influence this book may have had on us. It is one of the most exacting of all those published about the Aragonese genius. Since I was Sánchez Cantón's most assiduous student and collaborator, in Madrid, for almost 20 years, I was lucky enough to be a witness to some extremely important Goya finds made by him which were included in this and later studies. Let these words express my gratitude and honor his memory.

2. **Antecedentes, coincidencias e influencias del arte de Goya**, p. 24.

3. **Op. cit.**, p. 27.

4. Charles BAUDELAIRE: **Pequeños poemas en prosa. Críticas de arte.** Buenos Aires, Espasa-Calpe argentina, Col. Austral, 1948, p. 142. It should be noted that the commentaries on Goya appear in a chapter on «Some Foreign Caricaturists» in which Goya is considered «a singular man (who) has extended the horizons of the comic element.»

5. **Op. cit.**, p. 330.

6. Probably except for Picasso, no painter so repeatedly awakens the interest of critics and art historians. This makes it extremely difficult to compile an exhaustive bibliography.

7. The case of Ortega is especially representative. He was attracted above all to Velazquez and Goya because their works were an important means for discovering their complex modes of existence. For our artist, see the anthology published under the title **Goya**, in the collection «El Arquero,» Revista del Occidente, 3.ª ed., Madrid, 1966. Outside of Spain, an interesting work is that by F. D. KLINGENDER: **Goya in the Democratic Tradition,** with an introduction by Herbert Read, New York, Schocken Books, 1968, in which the Marxist sociologist tries to discover, through Goya's works, the political, economic and social conflicts of his time.

8. See, above all, the studies by the Marquis of Lozoya y Milicua about this trip. His journey through France is also interesting and has been described by various critics, especially Sánchez Cantón in the work mentioned.

9. Anyone interested in hearing Goya's activities as a tapestry cartoon artist discussed step by step should consult the magnificent monograph by Valentín de SAMBRICIO: **Tapices de Goya,** Madrid, 1946.

10. Goya's complete correspondence has not yet been published, but a repertoire of texts which continues to be very useful is the **Colección de 449 reproducciones de cuadros, dibujos y aguafuertes de Don Francisco de Goya precedidos de un epistolario del gran pintor y de**

las noticias biográficas publicadas por Don Francisco Zapater y Gómez en 1860, Madrid, Ed. Saturnino Calleja, 1924. Besides the curious texts taken from various authors collected there, these should be completed with others published later. The one mentioned here is cited by Sánchez Cantón, op. cit., p. 21; the petition which was denied is discussed by Sambricio, op. cit., doc. 60, p. XXXIII.

11. See Enrique LAFUENTE FERRARI: Las ideas estéticas de Goya, «Revista de Ideas Estéticas,» 1946. The study was reprinted in the work, Antecedentes, coincidencias e influencias..., pp. 318-330.

12. Op. cit., p. 31.

13. Goya, sus enfermedades y sus médicos. «Sinergia,» núm. 2, Barcelona, 1958.

14. The texts quoted and other interesting ones, as well, which we cannot quote here, may be seen in Ezquerra del Bayo's monograph and in Vida y obras de Goya by Sánchez Cantón, pp. 53-58.

15. The falseness of the date on the letter to Zapater was pointed out by D. Pedro Beroqui. Sánchez Cantón details the circumstances of the trip to Sanlúcar in an article published in 1928 in the «Boletín de la Sociedad Española de Excursiones.»

16. The circumstances related to the Duchess' death and the tests done on her remains are discussed in works by BLANCO SOLER: Esbozo psicológico, enfermedades y muerte de la Duquesa María del Pilar Teresa Cayetana de Alba, Madrid, 1946, and BLANCO SOLER, PIGA PASCUAL and PEREZ DE PETINTO: La Duquesa de Alba y su tiempo, Madrid, 1949, with curious and macabre details.

17. Information of great interest about Goya's property was brought to light by Sánchez Cantón in his long study, Cómo vivía Goya. I. El inventario de sus bienes, 1946.

18. For an extensive discussion of this picture, we recommend the consultation of Xavier de SALAS' monograph: La familia de Carlos IV, Barcelona, Ed. Juventud, 2.ª ed., 1959.

19. See the important monographic study by E. LAFUENTE FERRARI: Goya. El 2 de mayo y los fusilamientos, Barcelona, Ed. Juventud, 1946. This book, however, alludes to a text by Antonio de Trueba whose falsity was later demonstrated by the discovery of documents concerning the purchase of the Deaf Man's Villa which we cite in the next footnote.

20. See F. J. SANCHEZ CANTON: Cómo vivía Goya. II. Leyenda e historia de la Quinta del Sordo, «A. E. A.», 1946.

21. For an overall evaluation of Goya as a religious painter and a specific analysis of these last paintings, see the study by F. J. SANCHEZ

CANTON: **Goya pintor religioso,** «Revista de Ideas Estéticas,» 1946.

22. **Las pinturas negras de Goya en la Quinta del Sordo,** Milano, Rizzoli,
1963. An extremely concise synthesis of what is written in this very
expensive and luxurious edition may be found in the work by F. J.
SANCHEZ CANTON: **Goya: la Quinta del Sordo.** Col. Forma y Color,
Albaicín-Sadea Editores, 1966.

23. **Precisiones sobre la Tauromaquia, Las estampas inéditas de la Tauromaquia** and **Ilustración y elaboración en la Tauromaquia de Goya,**
«A. E. A.», 1940, 1941 and 1946, respectively.

24. See F. J. SANCHEZ CANTON: **Goya refugiado.** «Goya» Magazine,
1954.

25. See Manuel NUÑEZ DE ARENAS: **L'Espagne des Lumières au Ro-
mantisme.** Paris, Centre de Recherches de l'Institut d'Etudes Hispa-
niques, 1963. Various studies on this subject are published in this
volume.

BIBLIOGRAPHY

It is practically impossible to list, even in synthesis, the fundamental publications about the artist. In spite of its numerous omissions, very useful is the work by Agustín Ruiz Cabriada: *Aportación a una bibliografía de Goya*, Madrid, Biblioteca Nacional, 1946, which contains references to the most important publications up to the 200th anniversary of the artist's birth. Among the very many general monographs published afterwards must first be mentioned the one, so often cited in our text, by Sánchez Cantón: *Vida y obras de Goya*, Madrid, Ed. Peninsular, 1951; followed by the much more recent ones by Pierre Gassier and Luliet Wilson: *Vie et œuvre de Francisco de Goya*, Paris, Editions Vilo, 1970, and by José Gudiol: *Goya*, 4 vol., Ediciones Polígrafa, Barcelona, 1970. The work by E. Lafuente Ferrari: *Antecedentes, coincidencias e influencias del arte de Goya*—the illustrated catalogue for the exhibition held in 1932 by the Sociedad de Amigos del Arte, but published in 1947—is of great importance. Numerous and important works about the artist have been published in «Archivo Español de Arte» by Diego Angulo Iñiguez (1940, 1948, 1962), Lafuente Ferrari (1940, 1941, 1946), Marquis of Lozoya (1956), Xavier de Salas (1968), Sánchez Cantón (1929, 1931, 1946, 1947, 1952). Very useful are the monographic numbers dedicated to the artist by the «Revista de Ideas Estéticas» (1946) and «Goya» (1971). The work by Valentín de Sambricio: *Tapices de Goya*, Madrid, Patrimonio Nacional, 1946, is fundamental for the tapestries; for the engravings in general, see the book by Tomás Harris: *Goya Engravings and Lithographs*, 2 vol., London, Faber and Faber, 1964; for «Los Caprichos» see the monographic studies by Sánchez Cantón (Barcelona, Instituto Amatller, 1949) and López Rey (Princeton, 1953); for «The Disasters of War» see the monograph by Lafuente Ferrari (Barcelona, Instituto Amatller, 1952) and for the «Proverbs» or «Los Disparates» see the studies by Camón Aznar (Barcelona, Instituto Amatller, 1952) and Xavier de Salas (Barcelona, Gili, 1968). Among the many works on the drawings, let us recall those by Malraux: *Dessins de Goya au Musée du Prado*, Geneva, Skira, 1947; López Rey: *A Cycle of Goya's Drawings*, London, Faber and Faber; and especially, Sánchez Cantón: *Museo del Prado. Los dibujos de Goya*, 2 vol. Madrid, 1954, and Gassier: *Dibujos de Goya. Los albumes*, Preface by Xavier de Salas, Barcelona, Noguer, 1973. Goya's most important decorative job was studied by Lafuente Ferrari and Stolz: *Goya, los frescos de San Antonio de la Florida*, Geneva, Skira, 1955. This extremely brief list may be completed by checking the numerous references to books and articles in the bibliographical section of the «Archivo Español de Arte.»

BLACK AND WHITE ILLUSTRATIONS

PLATE 1. THE SLEEP OF REASON PRODUCES MONSTERS.—Prado Museum.—Drawing in sepia ink. Etching and aquatint. 216 × 152 mm., datable between 1797-98. This composition was going to be used as the cover for the series of «Los Caprichos,» but was finally assigned the number 43. Besides the engraving, two preparatory drawings with variations are preserved. Without discussing differences, let us emphasize the principal motif: the artist face down on a table, surrounded by owls, bats and other animals and with human faces floating in space... In the text we read: «...The author dreaming: his only intent is to banish harmful vulgarities and with this work, «Caprichos», perpetuate the solid testimony of truth.»

PLATE 2. EVEN THAT WON'T HELP YOU KNOW HER.—Prado Museum.—Drawing in sepia ink with India ink wash. Aquatint, with variations in the background figures. 200 × 150 mm. «Capricho» N.º 7, datable between 1797-98. To interpret the meaning of the scene, there is nothing better than Goya's own commentary: «How can he know her? To see her for what she is, glasses aren't enough; one needs judgement and worldly experience—and this is precisely what the poor gentleman lacks.»

PLATE 3. TOOTH HUNTING.—Prado Museum.—Sanguine ink etching and aquatint. 218 × 151 mm. «Capricho» N.º 12, datable between 1797-98. The brutal scene is illuminated by the following commentary: «The teeth of hanged men are extremely effective for casting spells; without this ingredient no success can be obtained. It's a shame the common people believe such idiocies.»

PLATE 4. BACK TO HIS GRANDFATHER.—Prado Museum.—Drawing in sanguine ink. 215 × 150 mm. «Capricho» N.º 39, datable between 1797-98. It is interesting to observe that an ass is the protagonist of several scenes in this cycle, and almost always with the animal in a seated position. As in other cases, the commentary is worth noting: «The Genealogists and Kings of the coats-of-arms have driven this poor animal crazy. And not only him.»

PLATE 5. THE INDISCREET MIRROR: THE CAT-MAN. ALGUACIL ARCHER OU SARGEANT.—Prado Museum.—Drawing in sanguine ink. Datable between 1797-98. This forms part of a group, with 3 others, treating the theme of mirrors, and which were surely done to be included in the series of «Los Caprichos,» though they were never etched. It has an almost illegible caption.

PLATE 6. THE CHINCHILLAS.—Prado Museum.—Drawing in sepia ink. Etching and aquatint. 208 × 151 mm. «Capricho»

N.° 50, datable between 1797-98. The drawing for this strange composition is very simple. The scene's meaning is cleared up somewhat by the text: «he who hears nothing, knows nothing, does nothing, belongs to the numerous family of the chinchillas, which never has been good for anything.» On this topic, see the study by Edith HELMAN (*Jovellanos y Goya*, Madrid, Taurus, 1970, pp. 183-199).

PLATE 7. SWALLOW IT, DOG.—Prado Museum.—Drawing in sanguine ink. Etching and aquatint. 217 × 151 mm. «Capricho» N.° 58, datable between 1797-98. The composition and commentary are sufficiently expressive: «Whoever lives among men will inescapably be tormented; if he wants to escape, he'll have to go live in the hills, and when he's there, he'll discover that living alone is also a torment.»

PLATE 8. MARTINACHO'S DARING IN THE ZARAGOZA BULL-RING.—Prado Museum.—Drawing in sanguine ink. Etching and aquatint. 245 × 355 mm. N.° 18 of «The Tauromaquia,» datable c. 1815-16. The scene, so expressive, needs no commentary. The main variation noted between the original drawing and the engraving is the presence of a figure climbing over the barricade, while in the etching the spectators are seen.

PLATE 9. MANLY COURAGE OF THE FAMOUS PAJUELERA IN THE ZARAGOZA BULLRING.—Prado Museum.—Drawing in sanguine ink. Etching and aquatint. 250 × 350 mm. N.° 22 of «The Tauromaquia,» datable c. 1815-16. The scene is distinguished by a lack secondary elements and the vigorous charge of the bull, contrasted to the horse's passivity.

PLATE 10. BULLBAITING.—Prado Museum.—Drawing in sanguine ink. Etching and aquatint. 245 × 350 mm. Datable c. 1815. The engraving resulting from this drawing forms part of a series of 7 plates which Goya never published in «The Tauromaquia» and which were printed for the first time in 1876. The scene is resolved with a profound feeling of movement, with the pack of dogs relentlessly pursuing the horned beast.

PLATE 11. THE FOLLY OF FEAR.—Prado Museum.—Drawing in sanguine ink. Etching and aquatint. 245 × 350 mm. N.° 2 of the «Proverbs,» datable betweeen 1815-24. With its date and subject matter, this and other scenes in the cycle bring us close to the hallucinatory world which predominates in the Black Paintings.

PLATE 12. WHAT LOVE CAN DO.—Prado Museum.—Drawing with India ink wash. 205 × 143 mm. This forms part of the same album to which N.° 15 belongs. The earlier number 26 is changed to 27. Though the meaning of the scene is not very clear, the plastic vigor and energetic volumes of the figure should be emphasized.

PLATE 13. BETTER TO DIE.—Prado Museum.—Drawing with washes in sepia and India ink. 205 × 142 mm. Part of the same album of drawings represented by illustrations 12 and 15. This one, with the number 13, appears along with other drawings of torture victims. It has been supposed that they refer to people persecuted between 1814 and 1820 by Ferdinand VII (Gassier).

PLATE 14. BECAUSE SHE KNEW HOW TO MAKE MICE.—Prado Museum.—Drawing in sepia ink. 205 × 144 mm. Datable between 1814 and 1820. On the figure's clothing may be read: «Because she kept on talking they gagged her and clubbed her on the head. I saw her, Orosia Moreno, in Zaragoza. Because she knew how to make mice.» It is part of a series of 48 drawings in which the artist, with the War of Independence over, reflects his reaction to the unbridled persecution during the absolutist years of Ferdinand VII.

PLATE 15. SO USEFUL MEN USUALLY END UP.—Prado Museum.—Drawing with India ink wash. 206 × 143 mm. No date. This belongs to a collection of drawings whose numeration in some cases, such as this one, was corrected by the artist himself —the original number, 16, was changed to 17. Due to its expressionist elements it was probably done after the War of Independence.

PLATE 16. I'M STILL LEARNING.—Prado Museum.—Pencil drawing, 191 × 145 mm. It forms part, with the number 54, of an album divided up among the Prado and other collections. This could conclude the entire cycle of Goya's production, though the old man's figure recalls one appearing in the series of the Black Paintings. It is possible to say, using Sánchez Cantón's words, that this «old man, bent with age, limping and having to support himself on two canes to be able to walk, but with a still scrutinizing look...» could serve as the best summary of Goya's prolific life.

COLOR PLATES

PLATE I. THE PARASOL.—Prado Museum.—Oil on canvas. 104 × 152 cm. Delivered August 12, 1777, for use as a model for a tapestry to decorate the Prince of Asturias' dining room in the Pardo Palace. In this painting Goya reduces the anecdotal element to a minimum, almost completely eliminating landscape and concentrating in the composition on the couple in the foreground. Chromatically daring is the theme of the parasol, although its shadow on the woman's face goes almost unnoticed. The little dog, on the woman's lap, is above all a dark spot of color serving as a counterpoint to the light hues which invade the lower part of the canvas.

PLATES II-III. BLINDMAN'S BUFF.—Prado Museum.—Oil on canvas. 269 × 350 cm. The sketch for the painting, in the same museum, measures 41 × 44 cm. Since this canvas was delivered to the tapestry factory early in 1789, it must have been done, in accordance with Sambricio's observations, the previous year. Few compositions in the cartoon cycle achieved such fame as this one. The distribution of the figures in a circle and the vibrant colors of the execution are, in fact, quite fortunate and original. Nonetheless, a certain disdain for individual characterization may be observed since the faces are, in the majority of cases, inexpressive, as if they were mannequins; perhaps the most sucessful element is the contrast of the postures. The variations between the sketch, the cartoon and the finished tapestry are interesting.

PLATE IV. THE DUCHESS OF ALBA.—Liria Palace, Madrid.— Oil on canvas. 194 × 130 cm. In this magnificent painting may be read the following dedication: «To the Duchess of Alba, Francisco de Goya 1795.» Cayetana's figure, though a bit rigid, possesses an irresistible charm. The Duchess' facial features, heavy eyebrows and tightly compressed lips, are concisely depicted with a somewhat stiff expression. The representation of the drapery is admirable and not lacking are certain humorous elements, such as the red ribbons which the Duchess wears on her bodice and in her hair and which match one adorning the paw of a little poodle at her feet. In the shallow landscape in the background we once more find a lack of interest in the study of nature, but this time certain Velazquez-like qualities are seen in the handling.

PLATE V. THE MARQUISE OF LAZAN.—Liria Palace, Madrid.— Oil on canvas. 193 × 115 cm. This work has no date, but due to stylistic reasons may be placed around the beginning of the 19th century. Of high quality, it displays a preoccupation with the light, which shines directly on the figure, thus making it stand out vigorously from the background. The textures of the draperies are notable. The subject, María Gabriela Portocarrero y Palafox, married to the Marquis of Lazán, was the aunt of the Empress Eugénie. The painting was left by this latter to the House of Alba.

PLATES VI-VII. THE FAMILY OF CHARLES IV.—Prado Museum.—Oil on canvas. 280 × 336 cm. This extremely famous picture was painted in Aranjuez in the spring of 1800. Thanks to a recent and most fortunate restoration, today the painting may be enjoyed, appreciating its rich coloring and discovering shades and motifs which had previously been forgotten. The work marks a high point in Goya's artistic trajectory and serves as a counterpoint to Velazquez' *Las Meninas*. The figures are spread out in a line across the width of the canvas. From left to right appear D. Carlos María Isidro (who would become a pretender to the throne on his brother's death, giving rise to Carlism); Goya, in a background self-portrait; the Prince of Asturias, the future Ferdinand VII, who moves toward the viewer; D.ª María Josefa, the King's sister, who would die the following year; an unidentified figure, who perhaps appears with her head turned to make an abstract allusion to the Prince's bride-to-be; the Infanta María Isabel, the monarch's daughter, who would marry in December of 1802, at the age of 13; Queen María Luisa, who holds by the hand her youngest son D. Francisco de Paula, whose tears would be the immediate cause of the tragedy of the 2nd of May; Charles IV, who has behind him his brother, the Infante D. Antonio and his eldest daughter, Carlota Joaquina, whose profile peeks out; finally, the Prince and Princess of Parma and Monarchs of Etruria (she being Charles IV's daughter), D. Luis de Borbón and D.ª María Luisa, holding in her arms their child D. Carlos Luis. Alongside these figures can be placed a second self-portrait of Goya, if we take into account that the canvas' restoration brought to light another image of the artist.

Although the distribution of the figures denotes a certain rigidness, it cannot be denied that they are very ably placed, each one linked to the next in a masterful fashion. There is no fixed rule for placing the figures, which form a compact group with Ferdinand VII at its head on the left; the monarchs, with the younger children, are comfortably spread out in a slightly oblique line, while the remaining figures are packed together in a diagonal further back. The two paintings which cover the wall in the background add a definitive note of color in appropriate contrast to the extremely rich coloring of the drapery on the main figures. As a historical document the picture seems to contain a subtle satire on the royal family, especially the monarchs, who preside over this odd ensemble of beings isolated from each other. Seldom has the loneliness felt by each member of a group been so thoroughly conveyed.

PLATES VIII-IX. WITCHCRAFT SCENES.—Lázaro Galdiano Museum, Madrid.—44 × 31 cm. and 45 × 32 cm. These two tiny pictures were painted for the Alameda de Osuna in 1798 and display, in the medium of oils, a thematic parallel with subjects more extensively developed in «Los Caprichos,» a strictly contemporary set of engravings. Probably referring to this fact, Camón says that «they answer the question, posed so often, of how to imagine what those enigmatic etchings would be like in color. Goya's imagination, spilling over in those years into the areas of criminal magic and horrendous masks, creates here scenes which mirror diabolical intentions, a subhuman world of vampires and witches' sabbaths...» Each scene serves as an early abstract of a motif which would achieve its more concrete development 20 years later—though with time the expressionist content of these subjects would increase.

PLATES X-XI. THE NUDE MAJA.—Prado Museum.—Oil on canvas. 97 × 190 cm. The famous paintings of the Maja lack dates; they appear documented for the first time in 1807, in Godoy's inventories. Sánchez Cantón, basing himself, among other things, on their stylistic similarities to *The Marquise of Santa Cruz*, believes the pictures to be from the same time, 1805. They are canvases of enormous pictorial interest, even discounting as improbable the hypothesis that they portray the Duchess of Alba. Along with the *Rokeby Venus* by Velazquez, the *Nude Maja* is, thematically speaking, exceptional in the panorama of Spanish painting. Goya offers us a direct and spontaneous version of the model, in spite of the artificial insertion of the head on the trunk, as Sotomayor has observed; in the *Nude Maja* is anticipated the boldness of Manet's *Olympia*. In the *Dressed Maja* we once again praise the freedom of the brush strokes which manage to exalt the textures of the drapery which clings tightly to the body.

PLATE XII. THE DRESSED MAJA.—Prado Museum.—Oil on canvas. 95 × 190 cm. See the commentaries for Plates X-XI.

PLATE XIII. THE BURIAL OF THE SARDINE.—San Fernando Academy Museum, Madrid.—Oil on wood. 82 × 60 cm. Datable during the war years, between 1808-14. The carnival scene is portrayed with rapid brush strokes which know how to reflect the animation of the popular festival. The group of dancers in the center of the composition stands out due to its bold feeling of movement.

PLATE XIV. THE DUKE OF SAN CARLOS.—Zaragoza Museum.—Oil on canvas. 280 × 125 cm. The picture could have been painted immediately after the War of Independence and would therefore be, stylistically, a companion to those of Ferdinand VII. It is a piece with extremely rich brushwork. A study of the head is preserved in the Collection of the Countess of Villagonzalo and a smaller version of the full-length portrait is in the Collection of the Marquis of Santa Cruz. The subject played an important role in Spanish political life, close to Ferdinand VII, and he took part in the investigation of Goya's loyalty. This portrait could be the fruit of his favorable attitude toward the artist.

PLATE XV. LEANDRO FERNANDEZ DE MORATIN.—San Fernando Academy Museum, Madrid.—Oil on canvas. 73 × 56 cm. There is a document stating that the portrait was being painted on July 16, 1799. It is an admirable testimonial to the famous writer and friend of the artist who would leave us information of prime interest about the artist's final years in Bordeaux; with its brownish tones, the coloring is somewhat somber, though the light projected onto the face helps emphasize the physical features and the psychology of the subject.

PLATE XVI. A SMALL TOWN BULLFIGHT.—San Fernando Academy Museum, Madrid.—Oil on wood. 45 × 72 cm. Like Plate XIII, the picture was probably done during the War of Independence (1808-14). In this tiny panel we see the painter of the «bravura style,» applying the term literally. The work is masterful, not only due to its thematic interest but also due to its technical elements. The calligraphy used to outline some figures expressed with splotches of color is surprising. The composition emphasizes the various planes, with the backs of the spectators in the foreground, the protagonists of the «fiesta brava» in the middleground and the silhouettes of the people grouped in the background and behind them, the shapes of some houses.

PLATE XVII. THE MADHOUSE.—San Fernando Academy Museum, Madrid.—Oil on wood. 45 × 72 cm. Like the preceding work, probably done during the War of Independence (1808-14). The scene, filled with nudes, reflects a great preoccupation with lighting effects and light colors. The spectacle of the unfortunate paranoids possesses a moving plastic forcefulness.

PLATE XVIII. PENITENTS' PROCESSION.—San Fernando Academy Museum, Madrid.—Oil on wood. 46 × 73 cm. Like the previous pictures, probably painted during the War of Independence (1808-14). The scene, interpreted with a moving expressionist feeling, seems dominated by the presence of the naked and bleeding backs of the penitents. The figures dressed in mourning serve as a chromatic counterpoint, while the images, crosses, standards and gas lamps help to define the spatial planes.

PLATE XIX. THE PICADORS.—Prado Museum.—Oil on wood. 23 × 40 cm. The detail reproduced belongs to a small undated picture which, nonetheless, should for stylistic reasons be placed in the final decade of the artist's life. Comparing the handling of this scene to the one in the San Fernando Academy, an even greater speed of execution and heavier impasto in the brushwork can now be seen. The group made up of the picadors and the bull stands out due to its exceptional plastic forcefulnes.

PLATE XX. THE CHARGE OF THE MAMELUKES AND THE IMPERIAL GUARD IN THE PUERTA DEL SOL.—Prado Museum.—Oil on canvas. 266 × 345 cm. With the canvas which follows, this constitutes the most vibrant and direct version of the tragic events experienced by the people of Madrid at the beginning of the War of Independence. Taking into account its documentary value, it was believed that Goya had been a witness to the scene. Without totally rejecting this hypothesis and recalling the sketches which are preserved, it is important to remember that the work should be dated around 1814, six years after the events portrayed. We should not forget the information supplied by Beruete that this painting and its pendant were used to decorate a triumphal arch built in honor of Ferdinand VII when he made his entry into Madrid on May 7th. *The Charge of the Mamelukes...* captures the attack against the French mounted troops as if it had been caught in a «snapshot.» The horror of battle, with sabres wounding men and animals, is perceived in a fierce manner, while the groups are scattered with a disorder surpassing all academic limits. Goya anticipated the chromatic effects, achieved by juxtaposing the shades instead of blending them, and modified the real colors (notice the horse with the green head) to satisfy strictly pictorial needs.

PLATE XXI. THE EXECUTIONS OF THE 3RD OF MAY (Detail). See the commentaries for Plates XXII-XXIII.

PLATES XXII-XXIII. THE EXECUTIONS OF THE 3RD OF MAY.—Prado Museum.— Oil on canvas. 266 × 345 cm. This painting merits the same comments in relation to the circumstances of its execution and chronology as *The Charge of the Mamelukes...* Nonetheless, the affirmation that the artist, along with his servant, saw the victims' bodies after the execution took place on Príncipe Pío Mount is no longer maintained. The scene is interpreted with a degree of drama unprecedented in the history of art. The exact moment when the condemned men are awaiting the rifle volley has been chosen and therefore time, reduced to a single instant, is filled with the terrible anguish of the wait. On the victim's faces is seen the terror of death, expressed in a special manner on each one of them. There is no exaltation of the dubious heroism of those who are fearless, but rather the much more human and intense heroism of those who die because they have no choice. The men facing the firing squad do not give their lives for their country: they are wrenched away from them. In view of this painful reality, the executioner's platoon lacks importance; it is seen from the back, like a shadow, with the light shining on the prisoners, especially the one in the center with his arms spread wide, whose white shirt and yellow pants match the colors projected by the lantern.

The mark left by this picture on artists from Manet (*The Execution of Maximilian*) to Picasso (*The Korean Massacres*) was decisive, not only with regard to its manner of interpretation of the theme and the composition, but also in its manner of vibrant light and color evaluations, in a precocious anticipation of Impressionism.

PLATE XXIV. PORTRAIT OF THE ARCHBISHOP COMPANY.— Prado Museum.—Oils. 44 × 31 cm. Study of the head for a full-length portrait done in the summer of 1790, as the result of a trip to Valencia, where the subject D. Joaquín Company was the archbishop. The fact that it is practically a sketch explains the singlular boldness of the coloring in this work and the forcefulness with which the expession, dominated by the prelate's penetrating stare, has been captured.

PLATE XXV. SELF-PORTRAIT.—San Fernando Academy Museum, Madrid.—Oil on wood. 51 × 46 cm. Signed in the lower left corner, «Goya, 1815.» It was donated to the Academy after the artist's death, by his son Francisco Javier. Together with a replica in the Prado, it constitutes a vibrant iconographical document of what Goya was like when he was about to turn 70. The light is concentrated on his head and the shirt which frames his neck. The diagonal posture is curious and is perhaps explained if we imagine the subject before the easel, twisting to look at himself in the mirror.

PLATES XXVI-XXVII. THE WITCHES' SABBATH.—Prado Museum.—Oil mural painting transferred to canvas. 140 × 438 cm. Done as part of the great cycle of the Black Paintings, between 1819 and 1823. The witches in their unholy assembly, with the He-goat at one side, form a crowd of bodies with horrible and misshapen heads turned in fright toward the animal in a monk-like habit which embodies the devil. The ultra-expressionist disintegration of the human forms reveals the radical changes Goya's taste had undergone when he crossed the threshold into old age. All explanations of the theme pale beside the testimonial value of this conglomerate of faces in which anguish reaches a state of paroxysm.

PLATE XXVIII. THE COLOSSUS OR PANIC.—Prado Museum.— Oil on canvas. 116 × 105 cm. An undated work, it is generally placed, for stylistic reasons, during the time of the War of Independence, identifying it as the painting *The Giant*, which was in the artist's possession in 1812. Sánchez Cantón imagines that Goya wanted to evoke the figure of Napoleon in the terrifying «colossus» which causes the confused flight of the figures, though the donkey, almost unnoticed in the foreground remains impassive. The dark colors and heavy impasto forecast the technique of the Black Paintings.

PLATE XXIX. SATURN DEVOURING HIS SON.—Prado Museum.—Oil mural painting transferred to canvas. 146 × 83 cm. Within the cycle of the Black Paintings, this composition occupies a unique position due to its cruel pathos and the symbolic meaning possessed by the mythological figure, expressing the passage of time. The splotches of blood which outline the victim's body add dramatic notes to this terrible scene.

PLATE XXX. THE PILGRIMMAGE TO SAN ISIDRO (Detail).—Prado Museum.—Oil mural painting transferred to canvas. 140 × 438 cm. The scene shows a handful of human beings heading for the saint's hermitage; standing out are disjointed faces which shout rather than sing to the sound of a guitar. There are also groups of cloaked figures, two men who are fighting and other people on different planes; the surroundings do not recall in the least the popular meadow. The theme, treated several decades before in the tapestry cartoon cycle, has now been converted into a spectacle colored with anguish by the pathetic voices of the pilgrims.

PLATE XXXI. TWO OLD MEN, EATING.—Prado Museum.—Oil mural painting transferred to canvas. 53 × 85 cm. From the cycle of the Black Paintings, like the others it displays the same chronological and stylistic elements. The subject shows a brutal vision of old age, with the old man on the right already prefiguring the idea of death.

PLATE XXXII. THE MILKMAID OF BORDEAUX.—Prado Museum.—Oil on canvas. 74 × 68 cm. One of the last works done by Goya and mentioned in a curious letter of Doña Leocadia Zorrilla's dated some years after the artist's death. The posture of this half-figure, conceived as a detail of a person mounted on a donkey, is surprising. More interesting is the coloring, heightened by vibrant touches of light, announcing new techniques of the octogenarian painter's.

El Autor soñando

PLATE 1

PLATE 2

PLATE 3

PLATE 4

PLATE 5

PLATE 6

PLATE 7

PLATE 8

PLATE 9

PLATE 10

PLATE 11

Lo q.e puede el Amor!

PLATE 12

Mejor es morir

PLATE 13

PLATE 14

Asi suelen acabar los hombres vtiles

106

PLATE 15

PLATE 16

PLATE I

PLATES II-III

PLATE IV

PLATE V

PLATES VIII-IX

PLATES X-XI

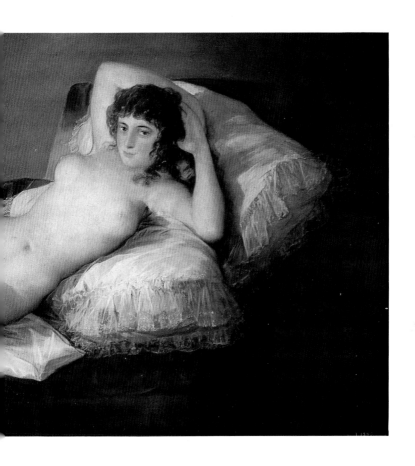

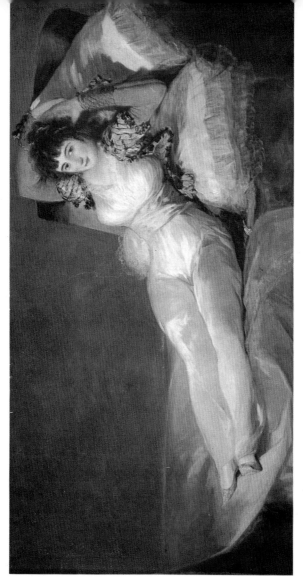

PLATE XII

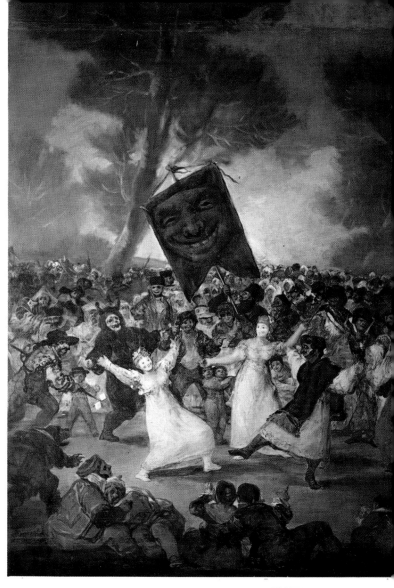

PLATE XIII

PLATE XIV

PLATE XV

PLATE XVI

PLATE XVII

PLATE XVIII

PLATE XIX

PLATE XX

PLATE XXI

PLATE XXIV

PLATE XXV

PLATES XXVI-XXVII

PLATE XXVIII

PLATE XXIX

PLATE XXX

PLATE XXXI

PLATE XXXII